From a Dream to a Drive

@ALWYNAL

Rollin' Into Life
After Work

Allyson Wynne Allen

ISBN: 979-8-218-57779-7 (paperback)
ISBN: 979-8-218-57778-0 (ebook)

First edition December 2024

Cover and Interior Graphics Designed by Kori Doran
Interior Edited and Designed by Danielle Anderson
and the team at Ink Worthy Books

Disclaimer

The information in this book is based on the author's knowledge, experience and opinions. The methods described in this book are not intended to be a definitive set of instructions. You may discover other methods and materials to accomplish the same end result. Your results may differ.

This book is not intended to give legal or financial advice and is sold with the understanding that the author is not engaged in rendering legal, accounting, or other professional services or advice. If legal or financial advice or other expert assistance is required, the services of a competent professional should be sought to ensure you fully understand your obligations and risks.

Contents

Dedication

This book is dedicated to my parents, Vivienne and Tony Wynne, for they instilled in me a sense of adventure and demonstrated what a vibrant retirement life can look like. My earliest and fondest memories are of us camping and traveling cross country. We went from pitching tents at lakes and rivers to driving across the country in an RV. After my brother and I were out of the house, they continued on with several cross-country road trips as well as traveling abroad. Thank you for your love and support and for giving me the means and desire to explore our world. Mom, you were taken from us way too soon. We miss you every day!

And to Harold, my husband and copilot, thank you for saying "yes" and being my road dawg!!

Foreword

It is my great pleasure to introduce *From a Dream to a Drive* by Allyson Wynne Allen, a book that encapsulates the essence of thoughtful retirement planning and the pursuit of one's dreams. Having known Allyson and her husband Harold as clients since 1998, I've had the privilege of witnessing their journey firsthand as they transformed their retirement aspirations into reality.

Throughout my career as a certified financial planner, I've consistently emphasized that successful retirement planning goes far beyond mere numbers: you should identify your life goals first, then you can focus on the numbers. This book exemplifies a holistic approach, embracing key principles that I believe are crucial for a fulfilling retirement.

First and foremost, one must determine their desired lifestyle before calculating their financial needs. This involves a deep dive into personal values, interests, and goals. One should take time to envision their ideal retirement, considering not just their financial requirements but also the quality of life they wish to achieve.

Equally important is the process of reflecting on one's passions and dreams. Retirement offers a unique opportunity to pursue long-held aspirations or discover new ones. Allyson and Harold's adventure is a testament to the rewards of following one's heart and exploring new horizons.

When it comes to choosing where to live in retirement, flexibility is key. It's perfectly acceptable, and often desirable, to consider multiple locations. Allyson and Harold's desire to relocate demonstrates how a change of scenery can invigorate one's retirement experience.

Another crucial aspect of retirement planning is considering the legacy one wishes to leave behind. This can involve financial bequests, charitable contributions, or passing on knowledge and values to future generations. The journey shared in this book is itself a valuable legacy that will inspire others.

I encourage all future retirees to create a bucket list of experiences, achievements, and adventures they wish to pursue. This provides direction and excitement and ensures that retirement years are filled with purpose and joy.

Lastly, it's essential to recognize the intricate connection between a happy mind and a healthy body. Retirement planning should encompass strategies for maintaining both mental and physical wellbeing.

From a Dream to a Drive promises to be more than just a retirement guide; it's a roadmap to a life well lived. Allyson's perspective, shaped by her own experiences and the financial guidance she and Harold have followed, offers readers a unique blend of inspiration and practical advice.

As you delve into this book, I encourage you to consider how you can apply these principles to your own life, regardless of where you are on your financial journey. Remember, a truly successful retirement is not just about financial security, but about creating a life that aligns with your deepest values and aspirations.

May *From a Dream to a Drive* serve as a guiding light on your path to a fulfilling future.

Alfred McIntosh, CFP®
Independent Fee-Only Financial Advisor

Introduction

When the opportunity to embrace "life after work" (or what many refer to as retirement) arose, it feels like my husband and I jumped right in. We quickly moved onto our next chapter of life, and I discovered so much about life after work in a short amount of time—three months to be exact! While our adventure began with a three-month cross-country trip (one that I invite you to join us on in this book), I want to encourage you to imagine what your life after work can look like. I decided to write this book to share our experience in hopes that it may be a source of inspiration and encouragement, moving you to look at where you are in your life and begin to consider what's next.

Are you just getting into adulthood, or maybe halfway through with kids away at college? Or maybe almost at the finish line? It is never too soon to start dreaming. What have you got to lose? Your dream just might come true!

When my husband Harold and I began our three-month adventure, I kept a journal and shared updates on Facebook, describing our journey and events along the way. Many of our friends and family enjoyed following along with us, especially as I posted at the end of each host location. We enjoyed the interaction with our followers as well. At the end of each post, I used hashtags that were meaningful to us—here's a few of our favorites:

#roadtrippin
#friendslikefamily
#thankfulgratefulblessed
#retiredlife

Our trip was an unforgettable experience, filled with memories and valuable lessons that I've been able to not only share with others but also take forward into my own amazing life after work. I never imagined I would be able to have it all in retirement. But I do, and you can too. I want to share my story with you with the hope that you, too, see the possibilities for your life after work.

I owe it all to God, who not only gave us this dream to explore His land but also graced us with the ability to plan and complete such a tour. You'll see that I've included a Bible verse at the end of each chapter to help highlight and summarize my thoughts and provide you with additional inspiration to reflect on.

Second, my gratitude goes out to Alfred McIntosh, CFP, best known as Mac, our financial advisor, who, from our earliest meetings with him, pushed us to aspire big and ponder the possibilities about our life after work. For every doubt and question we had, Mac had an answer. Outside of Mac, everyone else we told about our dream to go on this adventure thought we had lost our minds. While we had plenty of doubters, we carried on, confident in our decisions all along the way. Harold and I had worked hard for over thirty years, and now it was time to enjoy some of the fruits of our labor. Thank you to all of our hosts for caring for us out there on the road and allowing me to share a bit of our relationship in this book.

We traveled most of 2023, rented (mostly Airbnbs) in 2024, and, at the time of this writing, plan to purchase another home some time after that. We encourage all of our readers to dream big and not be confined to conventional thinking. Believe in the possibility of something great!

I invite you to come along with us on this road trip and watch for sparks of inspiration or places where your comfort zone might be asked to stretch. As I share some of my journal entries, I hope you come away with as much excitement as we felt leading up to the trip

Now let's roll!

Why Us, Why Now

By my mid-thirties, I was getting quite comfortable in my career. I had been on my job for nine years and was married with a one-year-old. I was making money and paying bills. Retirement was not on my radar; in fact, it was the furthest from my mind. What reason did I have to think about retirement at that age?

In a conversation with my friend and coworker, Kym, she suggested that I make an appointment with a financial advisor. We were earning a decent income and making adult decisions that go along with making money: home ownership, obtaining life insurance, establishing a college education account for our son, and investing in our companies' 401(k) accounts.

I didn't think I needed help, but I didn't know what I didn't know. An appointment was made. After all the pleasantries, Mac, the financial advisor, began to fire off all these questions about our income, where that money went each month, and what we wanted to do when our careers were over. I didn't know much beyond the general knowledge that we made enough to pay bills and put some into a savings account. I'm not much of a spender by nature, but it seemed prudent to know and understand where the money was going and why. What were we spending it on?

At that point, I didn't know about investments, stocks, or bonds or how any of that worked. And beyond a fleeting thought about a far-off destination in my career trajectory, I had not really considered retirement—it seemed so far off.

It took us weeks to gather all the information Mac was asking for. From that, he prepared an extensive "playbook" to get us from then to retirement. I stuck that in some file, and it eventually drifted out of focus as everyday life demanded so much of my attention. Mac continued to plant seeds about where we saw ourselves living in retirement. He wanted us to consider what we would be doing and where we'd like to live. At our annual meetings, he'd ask the same questions and encourage us to dream. He challenged us to expand our thinking and to be consistent with monthly deposits into our investment portfolio. He pushed us to look outside of our comfort zone, to think globally, and reminded us that we are limited only by our thoughts. Our relationship grew, and Mac became like family. We trusted his advice.

By now, Harold and I have known each other most of our lives. We've had good times and we've had our challenges. We managed the household together but we are also good at being quiet. At some point, I seemed to fall into autopilot. I was comfortable in my routine. We have two sons who are living out their own experiences. Avery, our oldest, went away to college, graduating in 2020 while the country was in lockdown from the COVID-19 pandemic. Harrison, our youngest, was wrapping up his tenth grade when the pandemic happened.

Just before this global crisis, I had started to think about leaving work. By that point, I had been with Kaiser for thirty years, and I was fifty-five years old, which is the earliest age one can retire from there. But leaving before the age of sixty-five would mean walking away from thousands of dollars each year in my pension, and I would have to pay for health insurance until I reach sixty-five.

As the world slowly shifted out of the pandemic and into the new normal, Harold and I were planning our next moves. We had been making monthly deposits in accounts managed by Mac for over two decades.

We knew we would retire in 2024, with Harold at the standard age of sixty-five, while I tried to make it until age sixty. I was getting tired, some of the patients I supported were changing, thanks to the internet—with so much information at their fingertips, parents can google their child's symptoms and come in requesting certain tests or medicine. It was a constant balancing act to educate the family while providing the best care possible to my patient. The workload, while always demanding, was still fulfilling. Then, suddenly, our life changed. Harold had a stroke in November 2021. It was the jolt that made us realize we needed to get on with the business of living.

Up until that point, Harold and I had traveled often and always planned to travel during our retirement. But at some point, that dream shifted into something much bigger: a drive across the United States.

While we had loved to travel, we didn't yet know if or where we would move once we retired. I did know, however, that I wanted to leave Los Angeles. The traffic was horrendous, homelessness was out of control, and I was ready to explore areas beyond Southern California. We considered relocating to other countries, as more and more people were heading outside the United States, for various reasons—some motivated by a lower cost of living, better health care costs, or better quality of food, all of which can lead to an overall improved quality of life.

Harold and I decided that we would first check out the US before heading abroad. There is so much to see right here "in our own backyard." After that, we would spend some time in a few different countries, with Dominican Republic and Portugal topping the list.

That was our initial plan, and we were excited to get started.

———

"Blessed are those who find wisdom, those who gain understanding, for she is more profitable than silver and yields better returns than gold."

Proverbs 3:13-14 (NIV)

2

Ready or Not,
It's Time to Go!

It all happened so quickly. The house went up for sale, and my last day of work was fast approaching. We didn't have long to finish packing, get rid of what we weren't taking with us, and hit the road. What started as an idea was now upon us. The pandemic, along with Harold's stroke, was my confirmation that we needed to get onto the next chapter of our lives. God had set it up, and Mac ran the numbers and gave the green light to pull the trigger on my retirement at age fifty-eight. Harold would not return to work after his stroke. I chose to work one more year, then hang up my stethoscope after thirty-three years of dedicated service as a pediatric physician assistant with Kaiser Permanente, Inglewood Medical Office. We know God ordained it, and Mac assured us that with my pension, upcoming Social Security payments, our 401(k), and the other accounts he had invested our funds in, we had more than enough to be able to live out our retirement dreams beginning January 2023.

What began as a vague fantasy to drive across the United States was shaping up with definite locations mapped out. Our route would be dictated by hitting points along the way where we knew people with whom we could stay. Most of our hosts were friends and family who had moved away from the Southern California area. You know how folks say "come and visit"; well, we took them up on their offer and they made good on it.

Now, I must confess, I really don't like to drive, especially long distances. It had always been challenging in that I would get what some call "the eyetis." Meaning, I would get sleepy very quickly while driving. And following his stroke, Harold was not all that comfortable driving either. Growing up in Los Angeles, California, my family vacations had been road trips. These vacations entailed drives ranging from weekend getaways up to six-week-long cross-country treks. My father, Tony, would map out the trips, and then we would venture out in the camper and camp all along the way to our destinations to places like the Florida Keys, Canada, and many of America's national parks.

As I grew and had a family of my own, I continued this tradition, traveling with my family on numerous road trips from Los Angeles to nearby locations like San Diego, Las Vegas, Palm Springs, and Fresno. Growing weary of road trips, I began to prefer flying to destinations. Maybe I was burnt out from road trips or thought I had graduated to air travel. But I reached a point when I knew I'd be fine if I never took another road trip in my life.

But now, in our retirement, we knew we'd want to see and get a feel for each state, and it didn't seem possible to do except by road trip. Flying around and renting cars would be inefficient and too expensive. It was clear that we would have to drive, we would have to take our car, and I would be responsible for most of the driving.

The planning began, and a loose itinerary and timeline started taking shape. All of our hosts were mapped out and expecting us soon. We even got my dad involved, as he was the master at planning road trips. In addition to our numerous camping and long distance road trips as a nuclear family, in their retirement, he and Mom continued driving across the United States in their recreational vehicle, and also flying across the world. With his experience, he definitely helped us pull our dream all together.

For my last day of work, I chose a date just before the Christmas holidays. Our house went up for sale on December 1st, perhaps not the best time given the holidays. The housing market was softening, after the incredible rise in the Southern California real estate market. Properties had bidding wars and often sold for over asking price. Even with the favorable market conditions, I had been unable to wrap my head around a house sale any time sooner with so many other things going on. The proceeds from the house were projected to be less than if we had put it on the market just a few months prior, but I could only focus on so many things at a time. We planned to sell the house to add the proceeds to our retirement nest egg and rid ourselves of expenses and worries attached to home ownership as we ventured out to see the United States. It was very freeing not to be homeowners for a time.

Months prior, we had reached out to our hosts to see if our visit was coming at a good time for them, based on our spring timeline. We had a few "must dates," which put some structure to that timeline. All hosts were eager to have us stop by on this exploration. We kept them updated with details of our pending visit with them. As it turned out, they all loved on us, enjoyed having us, and didn't want us to leave. We ended up spending between two days and two weeks at each location.

We continued to pack and purge the house, keeping in mind that, with the limited space in our SUV, we had to pack light for this three-month road trip. With Harold already claiming precious cargo space for his golf clubs, I wasn't sure how we'd fit everything else! We were taking the southern route, knowing it would be warmer in the southern states February through May. I checked the weather app often, but we determined we would need to be prepared for all seasons. After all, we were going through Colorado in April, where snow late in the season is a real possibility, and it was!

As expected, we didn't have the rush of offers or bidding wars that had been going on until only a month or two before we put it on the market. After several weeks, we had received only one offer, which went nowhere. Our agent advised us to reduce the price and have another open house.

This was January, and Southern California was having a particularly heavy rainy season. On the day of the scheduled open house, substantial rain was forecasted. The storm arrived that morning, causing me to question whether or not the open house should proceed. Our agent advised us that we should. We accepted an offer from one of four to five groups to come through that day and went on to close the deal within days of our departure. During their open house tour, the soon-to-be new owners commented, "At least we know the roof is good!"

We firmed up our route and communicated with the initial set of hosts that our original departure date would be pushed back a week. We were definitely departing on February 14th, which gave us the necessary time to clear out the house, rehome Marco, our dog of twelve years, and load ourselves into our small SUV. It was finally time to embark on this cross-country adventure. Ready or not, here we go.

To commemorate this occasion, we snapped a photo and shared our excitement on Facebook.

We are transitioning from the work life to that of a retired life. Harold and I will start our three-month journey across the United States. We look

forward to seeing God's handiwork, visiting numerous family and friends who have moved away and taking notes on how others do retirement. Keep us in your prayers and we will keep you updated on our travels.

#roadtrippin
#friendslikefamily
#thankfulgratefulblessed
#retiredlife

We were officially nomads, ready for this great adventure, and we were so excited to do this road trip! I felt so free with no house and our kids, now young adults, off having their own lives. I looked forward to visiting all of our hosts from all the different areas of our lives. From the response we received on our Facebook post and support from friends and family, it was clear that most people shared our excitement. We did, however, get some negative feedback from some who didn't understand how we could just leave everything behind. For Harold and I, we knew it was time to go, to do something different, and enjoy our retirement earned from over thirty years of labor.

It was happening, and nothing could stop us!

Reflections

As you begin to think about priorities in your life after work, number one should be your health. Mind your health, because without good health, life can be challenging. Retire while you can still enjoy all the adventures you dreamed to have in your life after retirement. We all know people who died before being able to retire, or those who retire only to live a short time afterward.

Your house and material things are replaceable. Let them go, if needed, and make memories! If you are thinking about leaving your house to loved ones upon your death, know that there are other ways to part with your assets. We've learned from other families that leaving a house to family may lead to strife and division as recipients may not agree on the numerous details that go into homeownership. The more people the house is "left to," the greater the chance of disagreement. There is a lot of money and decisions involved with homeownership.

Have a plan for retirement. There's a saying that goes, "If you fail to plan, you plan to fail." We weren't going to fail at this. We had a plan, and we were excited about executing it. It's never too early to start planning for life after work!

"Commit your work to the Lord whatever you do, and your plans will succeed."

Proverbs 16:3 (NTV)

3

Valentines With the Vincents

Day 1: February 14, 2023

Our youngest son Harrison is nineteen today! 48,399 miles on the odometer. We left home about 10:30 a.m., hurried to get everything done. Cleared out the house, dispersed trash, including all the bulky items for pickup. We gas up at one of the neighborhood fuel stations then jump on the 405 freeway. Our mission is not only to see some of the United States but also: 1) ask hosts to share two things about their retirement experience, and 2) see where we may want to live next.

Arrived at Fairwinds, Oceanside for our 12:30 lunch and tour—very nice. Continued on to Carlsbad to visit Harold's family. There we sat around watching a documentary on the NFL, chatting it up Harold's parents and his brother Darius. We continued on to the Vincents in the Pacific Beach area of San Diego.

DAY 2: FEBRUARY 15, 2023

A restful day in Mission Bay at the Vincent home. It began with breakfast burritos at Konitos. Harold was going to eat half but ended up eating the whole thing. He's been trying to watch his diet since the stroke. We walked to Trader Joe's to grab a few groceries. Drove back, then walked to the bay and back. We relaxed outdoors in the sun, reading, writing thank-you notes, and sending out pics from the retirement party to some of my coworkers.

Knowing that it's okay to start anything new slowly, we eased into this extended journey. First stop was San Diego, typically almost a three-hour drive south from Los Angeles. We had a lunch appointment at a retirement community in Oceanside. Liking what we saw on a virtual tour, Oceanside had started out being one of our top retirement locations. My dream destination had always been beachfront property, ocean-view living. After all, water is my peace.

The directions to the Fairwinds Retirement Community took us way east. In other words, it was nowhere near the beach! Our appointment was with the same ladies who gave us the virtual tour several weeks prior. We were greeted in the lobby with a personal welcome sign and face masks. The pandemic was not that far behind us, and we were, after all, at a senior residential facility.

We seemed to have attracted some attention upon arrival. I originally thought it was because of the color of our skin, but later found out that we looked too young! We were asked by several residents if we were considering this location for our parents! Even though this place wasn't for us, it was helping to shape our ideal retirement situation.

The Vincents were our first host. Harold had met Kristen at Whittier College and later sang at their wedding. Our friendship with the couple has grown over the span of thirty or more years. We would go see their girls play basketball when they came north toward Los Angeles, and they would travel to watch our boys play football and baseball. We even attended their daughter's wedding.

We've visited the Vincents several times, watching their property evolve from gorgeous to spectacular. Not only are they a block away from Mission Bay, they also have a homey outdoor space that can cater to whatever mood or vibe you're going for. It has everything from a treehouse and picnic table to a jacuzzi and a firepit; they even have an office and vegetable garden to round out their compound.

Kristen postponed Valentine's dinner a day, giving us time to catch our breath. She invited other friends, for a total of six, and we dined on baked fish, pasta, salad, asparagus, and wine. Dinner conversation included this excursion of ours. Everyone was eager to share their opinion on where we should go and what we should see, and while we were grateful for the encouragement and creative ideas, we knew we'd continue on the path we had originally designed.

After spending two nights with Steve and Kristen, we headed 350 miles east to the Phoenix area.

Reflections

A good thing can always be improved.

The Vincent home has always been a spectacular double lot a block from Mission Bay. It's an artist's dream, and they continue to update it to perfection. Passersby often stop to take in the beauty of their home. Harold and I are fortunate to call them friends.

In addition to starting out slowly, find yourself a good fee-only financial advisor. Begin that relationship by depositing what you can manage reasonably into an investment account. It may be as little as ten to twenty dollars per paycheck, and then slowly increase that as you can. Add additional funds when you get a pay increase or a windfall of any kind. With compound interest, even a little bit can dramatically increase the return on your deposits over the years.

When considering what to do and how to build your dream retirement life, start by asking questions of those already retired. Look at how they are living. Are they thriving?

Ask your employer about their retirement package. When is the earliest you can leave, and what will you get, if anything? Many companies are moving away from pensions and encouraging personal 401(k) accounts.

Consider who you know who's moved away and has invited you for a visit. To our surprise, all of our hosts were excited to be part of this journey. Every time I asked if we could come down for a few days, the Vincents always tried to accommodate us. As with all of our hosts, we simply asked. Some were unable to have us, so we asked others. We have some wonderful friends and family.

———————————

"Until now you have not asked for anything in my name. Ask and you will receive, and your joy will be complete."

John 16:24 (NIV)

4

Friends In Phoenix

DAY 3: FEBRUARY 16, 2023

Spent the day driving from San Diego to Goodyear, Arizona. Harold took over driving for a while. We listened to gospel music for most of the ride, then I needed to dance to get energized so I put on some Michael Jackson. We arrived at Kym's exhausted. We had Panera for dinner (using a retirement gift card). I got a good night's rest—warm and comfy on the left side of Harold, my spot.

Day 4: February 17, 2023

We had a tour of Kym's complex—Robson Ranch. Walked through several model homes and saw the clubhouse equipped with a pool, gym, pickleball and tennis courts. We are early in our search. It's good to see this community.

I'm also learning what I don't want in my retirement home. Hers is called a fifty-five-plus active community—lots of activities and amenities. All houses look similar on the outside, some version of beige.

That's what we need to be researching: fifty-five-plus active communities, not retirement communities. We are getting educated.

We had dinner with Kym and Toni. Ended up at a Thai spot after going to several places that had over an hour wait. It was, after all, a Friday night and a holiday weekend at that.

Good food, good conversation, good night.

Mountains with greenery on rocky surfaces made up our scenery as we left California. And as we crossed into Arizona that afternoon, I was able to appreciate some differences between California and Arizona. Arizona is a desert! It's dry, brown, and flat with mountains in the distance. Driving east, we enjoyed watching the sun set as we approached the city of Goodyear.

Kym, my friend of thirty-five years, was our host in Arizona. She is who introduced us to Mac. She is a fellow physician assistant whom I met in Houston while I was there for a clinical rotation. We traveled the same educational path, but she was a few years ahead. We both attended the University of Colorado, Boulder undergrad, enrolled in the Child Health Associate Program (our physician assistant program), but it wasn't until I got to Houston when we finally met. Later, she moved to Los Angeles shortly after I returned home from Colorado after graduating.

She, too, was hired by Kaiser Permanente West Los Angeles about a month or so after I was. We were the very first and, to date, the only physician assistants hired in pediatrics. She retired several years prior and relocated to Goodyear, Arizona.

We had several friends to visit while in Arizona. The first was Toni, a friend through my mother, Vivienne. Mom and Toni met in the travel business and soon became running buddies. Over the years, Toni became one of Mom's dearest friends. Since she went by the same name as my dad, it was a running joke as to whom one was speaking of: Toni with the "i" or Tony with a "y."

Toni now lives in Sun City West, which is an entire city for residents over age fifty-five. Sun City West has no schools, so residents don't pay school tax as a line item on property taxes. We are learning all about being seniors and retired living. We want all the discounts, deals, and perks!

Maxine is another friend who moved to the greater Phoenix area from Los Angeles. She agreed to meet us for lunch the following day.

All of these friends shared highlights of their retirement. They are all actively involved in their community. Kym and Toni have joined clubs that interest them, and Maxine enjoys living in a walkable community. She may walk or ride her bike to run errands and enjoy her favorite restaurants.

Reflections

Be confident in your decision. When you work through the process of making a decision about something such as committing to your financial future or leaving your employer, be sure to do your due diligence and think it all the way through. As you cover all the bases, you'll feel confident with your choice.

The three ladies we connected with in Arizona all remain active in retirement. They are all happy with the timing of their retirement and also about moving away from Southern California. It seems to take some people longer to enjoy their retirement and

adjust to not working. Some have reported bore-
dom or feeling restless. I know many who return to
work after they have departed! This will not be my
issue!

———————

*"There is a time for everything, and a season
for every activity under heaven."*

Ecclesiastes 3:1 (NIV)

5

New Relationships In New Mexico

DAY 6: FEBRUARY 19, 2023

We left Kym about 7:45 a.m., gassed up, I got a Pepsi, and we rolled well for a while. This was going to be a long day of driving. We stopped several times, including lunch. Harold drove a little while so I could rest. I took a little cat nap.

Later on in the drive, I still had to pull off to doze. The drive turned out to be tougher than anticipated. We finally made it to Loree's beautiful adobe home in Corrales, New Mexico, a suburb of Albuquerque. She had dinner waiting for us. We had a lovely visit over a delicious meal.

Oh! What made the drive fun was being able to listen to Sunday church service. This was the last Sunday Bishop Ulmer would preach. Later we were able to watch the tribute concert.

DAY 8: FEBRUARY 21, 2023

We are having a great time with Loree. She has been a wonderful host. She gave up her owner's suite for us; she says because it has an adjoining bathroom. She lives here with her pets, Jill, a lovable boxer, and Johnny, a three-legged cat. She is a smart shopper. She buys at the big-box stores then breaks things down, freezing into single servings.

We had salisbury steak, taco salad, potato and egg breakfast, and avocado toast for Harold, his new favorite. We toured Old Town Albuquerque and Corrales. Weather is coming, Loree warns. She would love for us to stay but we press on.

Bishop Kenneth C. Ulmer was also "repositioning," as he put it. He was retiring from being the Senior Pastor-Teacher for over forty years at Faithful Central Bible Church, which has been our church home for over thirty years. Harold introduced me to this church shortly after we started dating.

There, we grew as adults and Christians. We raised our boys in this church. We made wonderful, life-long relationships there and are still very involved in various ministries. We were elated to participate, although remotely, in Bishop's final celebrations.

One good thing that came out of the pandemic was that all church services are now streamed online. We listened to his final sermon as we traveled east through the mountains of Flagstaff, Arizona.

The weather was crisp enough to maintain the patches of snow present on the hills adjacent to the interstate, a gorgeous backdrop to go with Bishop's final sermon as Senior Pastor-Teacher.

We were uplifted from his sermon on our way to our next host, Loree. I originally knew Loree through my parents, more from my dad. Mike, Loree's husband, worked with Pops at Fire Station 61. Loree and Mom became tight over time as the couples traveled several times together. Boy, do they have some stories of fun in sunny Mazatlan or skiing in Lake Tahoe, sometimes with about ten other firefighter couples.

Prior to our visit, I knew Loree only through stories told by my parents about these excursions, Super Bowl parties, and the times they visited her in Crestline, California, and Alpine, Wyoming.

Loree became my "road mom." She expressed, early and often, concern for our safety on the road and wanted to ensure our protection. She wasn't satisfied with the periodic social media posts, so we agreed to let her know each time we were hitting the road and again once we arrived at the next location. That worked for both of us.

Have I said how much fun this trip has been so far! This drive was extremely exciting and not as difficult as I had imagined. We enjoyed the sights and admired the vast open spaces in between communities ranging from very small to large cities. I looked forward to visiting the different states we would travel through and try to assess their livability. We knew that where we would end up must have some water (a lake or pool), golf, and be a smaller city with less people than Los Angeles.

Wherever it was, it wouldn't be in the heart of any city. We were ready to move out to the suburbs.

Reflections

Be excited for your future! Of course, be present in the here and now, but the future will be here before you know it.

I was extremely excited for our adventure! I'm so glad we chose to just go for it, but you have to be careful who you tell your dreams to. We got so many questions, and while I didn't always have all of the answers, I knew we were retired and had nothing but time to fill in the blanks. Time was ours to do with whatever our hearts had a mind to do.

What is it that you've always wanted to do? Do you have any dreams, aspirations, a hobby, or a side hustle you'd like to spend more time doing? Or how about a gift or talent you have been suppressing? Let loose in retirement.

Somebody needs you and your talent; spread your wisdom around. Be a mentor to someone entering your field. Be open to possibilities. I dream of teaching water safety once we are settled. That would be one of the ways I give back. I want everyone to know how to be safe in and around water.

After life happened and Loree wanted something different, she decided to check out three other states. Because of those moves, she has made more friends and had plenty more experiences than if she had stayed "on the mountain," as she puts it.

She has flourished in photography, submitting some of her favorites to many international websites. One of her photographs of her cat Johnny was recognized and printed in a national magazine!

"In his heart a man plans his course, but the Lord determines his steps."

Proverbs 16:9 (NIV)

6

A Whole Lot Happening In Texas

DAY 10: FEBRUARY 23, 2023

We arrived in Arlington, Texas, yesterday. A fairly long drive from Albuquerque; we split it up by spending one night in Amarillo, Texas. Harold drove some, but we both got nervous due to oncoming cars entering the two-lane Highway 287. Marilyn and Gary also opened up their home to us, insisting that we use their owner's suite equipped with one of those fancy beds that adjust like a hospital bed and a jacuzzi tub! They were in Chicago with their daughter, Gabby, and her family, who will be our host when we get to Chi-town. We are having great weather so far. We are outside by their pool, enjoying the fresh air and happy hour treats.

Mark, a former Major League baseball player, stopped by for a visit before we met Darryl and Tia for a Tex-Mex dinner. All are friends of Harold's from San Diego.

Great company, great conversation. Harold has many friends who have relocated from San Diego to the Dallas-Fort Worth area. We visited with as many as we could.

The following day we had lunch at Pappadeaux with the Manleys, another childhood connection from San Diego. We had a late visit from cousins Rachel and Gary. Harold was able to catch up on family news on his maternal grandfather's side—his New Orleans family.

DAY 13: FEBRUARY 26, 2023

We are now in Cypress, Texas, a suburb west of Houston. We traveled on small roads for a while and stopped at a "picnic area" for lunch. I was trying to visit a former patient, Taliyah, who attends Prairie View—she did not answer her phone. Killing some time, Harold and I got pedicures. Once we finally spoke, I learned Taliyah had slept until four that afternoon!

Vernon and Cheryl have been great hosts, so much so, we extended our visit to catch a couple of her school events.

DAY 15: FEBRUARY 28, 2023

It has been wonderful here in Cypress. Cheryl and Vernon have been awesome. We finally had a chance to visit with Taliyah. I took her to Walmart to restock her supplies. We ate at Pizza Hut only because it was close and we were beyond hungry. We attended the Cypress High School Black History program, which was amazing, followed by the boys basketball playoff game. They lost on the very last play in the very last second. What a heartbreak! Cheryl is the school's principal. She took us on a tour of her school. It looked like a small college—it was a huge *campus. I was impressed by their various vocational programs which have been cut from so many other school districts. They have thriving auto mechanic, cosmetology, culinary, and fashion design programs. All of these programs give students either a license or certification to be able to get jobs right out of high school. College isn't for everyone and that's okay. There are many pathways to reach one's goals.*

Our host in Cypress, Texas, Cheryl, is great at what she does. As we toured the school, it was clear that she is well-liked and respected by both students and staff. Texas public education was impressive; tax dollars at work!

It was great catching up with various sets of people while we traveled through Texas. We felt their love and excitement that we were in their town and were able to connect over a meal. Such great food in Texas!

At the last minute, someone from our church who had been living in the Dallas area for years and had been following our journey on Facebook sent me a message, hoping we could connect before leaving the area. Myra, a former church member, remembered Harold from the youth choir at Faithful Central. He had been an adult mentor in that choir and her daughter had been a member. That was nearly thirty years ago! We were able to meet Myra and her daughter, Tennille, for breakfast as we headed out of the Dallas-Fort Worth area. It was crazy how God orchestrated every step of every visit. Everything just fell into place so effortlessly.

Marilyn and Gary, our "ghost hosts" in Arlington, were our first hosts in the large state of Texas. They were also a connection through my parents. Mom met Marilyn while working at a travel agency. There they became close and traveled on countless business trips together. They were so dear to one another that Mom was Gary's "stand-in mother" at their wedding. Soon after they were married, Marilyn and Gary moved back to her home state of Texas.

Some time later, Mom was employed by American Airlines. As a benefit, employees and their family members were able to fly "non-rev," meaning non-revenue—these passengers were able to fly for little or no cost as space was available. However, there was a hierarchy. Being a dependent of the employee put me at the very lowest priority for boarding a flight. To fly home from college for winter and summer breaks, Denver to Los Angeles, meant going through Dallas. American Airlines had no direct flights. The route was Denver to Dallas-Fort Worth, then Dallas-Fort Worth to Los Angeles. Since Marilyn and Gary lived in Arlington, their home was the spot for layovers when no more seats were available. As a result, I spent many nights with Marilyn and Gary.

When we were planning this trip, I was not looking forward to driving through Texas. I remember riding through Texas as a little girl, and it seemed to take forever to get out of the state. As I recall, the drive was flat and dusty, and the scenery, dull and unappealing.

This time, perhaps because of our route or because I was an adult and "in the driver's seat," it was actually enjoyable. We didn't go straight across the state. Instead, we drove south, from Dallas to Houston. To my surprise, it was quite scenic. Green rolling hills dotted with cows and horses spanned the wide open spaces along Interstate 45.

Our first stop heading into the Houston suburb of Cypress was to Prairie View A&M University, a Historically Black college. There, I wanted to visit with Taliyah, a former patient I had followed for years. I cared for her and her brother as they grew up. Taliyah was now a freshman at Prairie View.

While visiting the campus, we caught some of a women's softball game. We also noticed the men's baseball team having practice. To our surprise, they had several White guys on the team. I was glad to see the integration but also wondered if they had taken opportunities away from qualified Black students.

We left campus and continued on to meet our next hosts, Vernon and Cheryl in Cypress. Harold knew

Vernon from their childhood days in San Diego. They got to know each other better when Harold began high school at Patrick Henry High where Vernon attended. They knew many of the same people, as did Cheryl and I. She and I are both from Los Angeles. We didn't know each other growing up, but Facebook revealed several mutual friends. We became fast friends, sharing our stories over dinners and walks.

As some hosts were still employed, we would venture out exploring on our own and ask for their advice as to what to see in their city. We would search for local sights and attractions. Carrying around a small computer disguised as a phone, one can easily find things to do anywhere. This device holds an abundance of information on a vast array of subjects. It provided us with knowledge and proved to be exact in giving us driving directions to any place. Woe to the one who loses their phone as our lives have become intertwined with this necessary appendage.

In the Houston area, we used the phone to find and hit a few tourist spots. The Buffalo Soldier Museum was insightful and well put together. The Waterwall was amazing. This iconic centerpiece of Houston was worth the drive. Its water spray was refreshing on an 83-degree day in February!

Reflections

It can take time to get into a rhythm. Life can run smoother if there's routine. If you feel disorganized and scattered, try to write down what you do day after day. Can you see a pattern, a routine? If not, be patient with yourself. As I got into future-thinking habits, it became second nature.

By the time we made it to Texas, Harold and I had gotten into our own rhythm. Even though Pops gave us sound advice such as hit the road early, we found ourselves having a more leisurely approach. We packed the car the night before and were ready to leave once up and dressed.

Since his stroke, Harold sleeps later and it takes him some time to get going. We just took our time getting on the road. We didn't want to feel rushed on this trip. We wanted to enjoy every minute of every location and host. We're retired, we have nothing but time.

We see some retirees who are grandparents and really thrive in that role. Marilyn and Gary are all in with their grandchildren. They have their fifteen-hour drive to see their grandkids down to a science. From Arlington, Texas, to Chicago, Illinois, is part of their routine. They go there that often. They love being a tangible part of their grandchildren's lives.

I know others who have delved into their talent to become authors, photographers, or teachers. Hopefully, one can enjoy their time in retirement and find purpose in this phase of life. We all work so hard obtaining an education, getting established in our career, and raising a family. Retirement can be our reward for putting in the hard work. You will find a new routine in your retirement as well.

Start dreaming now and find a really good financial advisor. I had no idea saving just $200 to $500 a month with our financial advisor would allow us to have such an exciting life in retirement.

———————————

"The wise man saves for his future, but the foolish man spends whatever he gets."

Proverbs 21:20 (TLB)

7

Lots to Do In Louisiana

DAY 17: MARCH 2, 2023

We arrived at Cousin Craig's yesterday. We will stay here a few days and then go to Cousin Tonyelle's for another several days. We met Bryant for lunch. He's Harold's friend from San Diego. Afterward I had to go buy some shorts. I only packed one pair of shorts and it has been unseasonably hot thus far.

Tomorrow there is a Davis family celebration for January, February, and March birthdays. We will go with Craig and see Tonyelle and everyone in this large extended family.

Day 20: March 5, 2023

We had breakfast at IHOP after the crowd at Ruby Slipper spilled out the door. Again we visited a car wash and hit the road to Slidell. Time to regenerate and get in touch with Jesus. Cousin Tonyelle's yard is awesome and a quiet place to hear from our Savior. I will cook dinner and surprise Harold with his favorite bean soup. His birthday is soon.

Day 25: March 10, 2023

We are now in Pensacola, Florida. We had a wonderful time with Tonyelle and her husband Kenneth; we love their home and neighborhood in Slidell, Louisiana. But while we were there, tragedy hit the extended family. A sixteen-year-old family member from Jonesboro, Georgia, suffered an aneurysm and, sadly, did not survive. Most of the aunties went from New Orleans to Atlanta to be with the affected immediate family. Understandably, it dampened the *mood and the remainder of our time in Louisiana. We carried on with celebrating Harold's birthday. Cousin Taylor came over when she got off work.*

As our adventure continued, we aimed east and crossed over into Louisiana. Vernon had warned us how different the roads would be. In Texas, the ride was smooth. Although the scenery was nicer to look at in Louisiana, Vernon was right—the roads were a bit rough. Continuing east, I was on alert for random potholes while admiring the tree-lined Interstate 10.

We arrived at Harold's cousin Craig's in Addis, Louisiana, a little southwest of the bridge on Interstate 10 leading in and out of Baton Rouge. This bridge is one of the only ways to get to and from Baton Rouge. Without knowing, we arrived in the thick of rush hour traffic. I was tempted to take an exit, hoping for a different route. Instead, we endured the traffic, only later to find out there had been no quicker alternate route to get to Craig's anyway.

The day after arriving at Cousin Craig's, he drove us to the West Bank area of New Orleans to attend the birthday celebrations for family members born in January, February, or March. What a wonderful family tradition. This large extended family is committed to coming together often. Distance doesn't matter. All of them will drive miles to get to a family gathering.

Visiting and meeting up with people continued. The next day, Bryant, a friend of Harold's from San Diego, took us to a Louisiana State University (LSU) baseball game. We thought we were in a major league stadium by its size and the number of fans. It was incredible! For March, it was unseasonably hot, and our seats were in the outfield on metal bleachers with nothing to shield us from the heat as we sat there. Harold and I seemed to be the only fans with no LSU gear on, but we were lucky that Bryant gifted us with LSU seat cushions and Harold a baseball cap. Harold had not packed a cap! Now we felt like official Tiger fans, while cushioning and cooling our buns. That team would go on to win the Men's College World Series a few months later.

We continued on to our next host in Louisiana to see another cousin, Tonyelle, and her husband, Kenneth. They live in Slidell. We opted to take Interstate 12 to Slidell and bypass the city of New Orleans and the Causeway. This is the bridge that hovers a mere fifteen-feet over Lake Pontchartrain for nearly twenty-four miles! I didn't think I would be scared, but we opted for the route without the bridge just in case.

They have a large ranch-style home with a huge backyard. We enjoyed their neighborhood. It was tranquil, away from the city with an abundance of trees. I enjoyed reading in the back yard and resting in the hammock they had set up. While in the backyard, Tonyelle received that dreadful call from Cousin Tedra in Atlanta saying her daughter Kayla fell at school, hit her head, and was being transported to the hospital. All of the extended family members went into prayer and many drove to Atlanta from New Orleans. But God decided to take Kayla home to Himself. She did not survive what turned out to be a brain aneurysm.

Before this tragedy occurred, we were able to visit Global Wildlife. It was exciting to get up close and personal with the animals. Global Wildlife mimics the wide open spaces where animals are able to roam freely. We watched kids feed the animals from their hands as we rode in an open-air shuttle.

Both hosts in Louisiana were cousins on Harold's maternal grandmother's side. I got to know Craig and Tonyelle and other family members better during our annual visits to Louisiana while our son was in college at Loyola New Orleans. This family had a huge reunion one summer where I was able to meet over 150 new cousins. On top of that, Mardi Gras in New Orleans was my dad's eightieth birthday request. We've enjoyed our times with family in NOLA.

Also while in the New Orleans area, I was able to catch up with another former patient, Alana, who gave us a tour of Xavier University. It was great to see and hear that she was doing well as an upper-classman. She was involved in student government and figuring out her next steps.

We also celebrated Harold's birthday in Louisiana. He golfed while I was able to spa a bit. Cousin Taylor stopped by for his birthday dinner and a quiet celebration. It was difficult with the sudden death of such a beloved family member.

Taylor is from Southern California. She recently got her nursing degree from Dillard University and was already in a nurse practitioner program. She told me a story of how she identified a pulmonary embolism on a postpartum patient when the resident doctor overlooked some of the signs. Go Taylor! This was wonderful to hear since women of color have a high mortality rate surrounding childbirth. The patient could have been a sad statistic had it not been for Taylor's clinical acumen.

Reflections

Life is an emotional experience, and it's wise to allow yourself to feel all the feelings. We can get into trouble when we try to avoid the feelings or numb our feelings with such distractions as eating, shopping, drinking, smoking, or gambling—or whatever your thing is. Instead, find healthy ways to process your emotions—go for a walk, exercise, talk to a friend or therapist.

By this point, we had been on the road almost a month and it was already so much fun—even better than how I imagined it would be. We were learning that while people thought we were completely crazy to roll out this big dream after work, they also admired what we set out to do. They wondered, who does this? Who sells their house and gets rid of most of their belongings to hit the road in their car for three months?

My main concern was for our two young adult sons. The oldest, Avery, having graduated from college in 2020, was still getting on his feet. Our youngest,

Harrison, was just starting his second semester in college in Denver, Colorado. I was torn. Do we stay in Los Angeles or do we live out this dream? Do we live our life for others, one of regret? Or do we live for ourselves first? It came down to Harold and I choosing us over everything else. His stroke made us behave with intention. We knew our parenting wouldn't end, and we continued to be involved in our sons' lives, although remotely. The nest was dismantled.

Tomorrow is not promised. It's an often-used saying, but true. Just look at the story of Kayla, whose life was cut short at just sixteen years of age. God called her home at the end of an ordinary school day. She had no preceding health concerns or warning signs. She had just spoken to her mother, asking for a ride home when the unthinkable happened.

Harold's stroke, although not fatal, started at midnight, disguised as a vomiting episode with no prior warning. Surviving that experience has helped us to see what was most important at this time in our lives. We were determined to live life fully each day.

———————

"How do you know what is going to happen tomorrow? For the length of your lives is as uncertain as the morning fog—now you see it; soon it is gone."

James 4:14 (TLB)

8

Passing Through Mississippi and Alabama

Day 26: March 11, 2023

Today we went through four states in about four hours on Interstate 10: Louisiana, Mississippi, Alabama, and Florida. We had a salad dinner with Cousins Jamie and Malique in Daphne, Alabama, and saw the USS Alabama.

While passing through Alabama, we were able to catch up with Cousin Jamie. She, too, is an off-shoot of the family of New Orleans. She and her son Malique moved from Northern California to Alabama in 2010. They seem to enjoy their town of Daphne, a suburb of Mobile. Jamie is fulfilled by her job in a middle school and also by being an incredible mom to her talented student-athlete son.

Leaving Alabama, we opted for the more scenic route. We hugged the coastline and drove through the Panhandle, moving our way toward Destin and Panama City, Florida. The scene as we approached looked like the white sandy beaches of the Caribbean or the Mediterranean. It was postcard spectacular! Tonyelle had mentioned that Destin was a favorite getaway for her and Kenneth, and we could see why. We grabbed some lunch to eat at a park while gazing out toward the Gulf of Mexico.

We continued on the coastal route until Panama City and then headed north to connect back to Interstate 10 for our overnight stay in Tallahassee.

The distance between our hosts in Louisiana and Florida was more than I wanted to drive in one day—two days was more than enough. We spent a hotel night in Pensacola and again in Tallahassee. We drove by the famous Florida State University on the way to dinner.

Driving and maneuvering around is so common nowadays. It may have been naïve of us to have started this trip without a proper, modern navigation system, although it seems like a 2018 Lexus would have had a factory-installed GPS. We did bring paper maps of all the states we planned to travel through, but upgrading our navigation system to Apple CarPlay while in New Orleans made a huge difference, as I was able to see where we were headed without looking at my phone or a paper map.

Having a visible map on the dashboard with clear, concise directions also made the excursion more interesting as we could see how many miles to go, how long it would take, and other helpful data points. I discovered a drive time app that gave me the mileage to our next location. That way I was able to determine if we would need to spend the night at a hotel before our next host.

Reflections

The atmosphere along the way was incredible. It was nothing short of amazing to see this great land up close and personal. I knew there was beauty to see right here in our own backyard!

Sometimes life requires you to step out of your comfort zone and make a move regardless of other's opinions and questions. If you can dream it, fund it, and are retired, you have very few reasons not to make it happen.

Or in Jamie's case, she made a decision she thought was best for her and Malique. Moving out of California was courageous of her—a bold move, as a young, single mother, that has proved to be positive for them. They are fond of their lifestyle there.

Follow your heart, seek wise counsel, think it through, and live with no regrets.

———————————

"Yes, be bold and strong! Banish fear and doubt! For remember, the Lord your God is with you wherever you go."

Joshua 1:9 (TLB)

9

Flying High In Florida

DAY 28: MARCH 13, 2023

From Pensacola, we stopped in Tallahassee. We didn't do much, had dinner from Black-owned Pinappetit, then went to Publix for groceries.

We arrived in Jacksonville last night at about 5 p.m. Since we were early for our hosts, we found a Costco nearby. We will be here for a week.

DAY 31: MARCH 16, 2023

We are enjoying Jacksonville and looking forward to seeing American Beach on Amelia Island. I was able to enjoy some self-care—Linda dropped me off to get my eyebrows shaped and a pedicure.

DAY 32: MARCH 17, 2023

Today I have some time alone. The guys are golfing. I am poolside braving the wind. I have so much to be thankful for. We have such good friends.

DAY 33: MARCH 18, 2023

Change in plans due to weather. We will see American Beach tomorrow. We will pack and plan to head to Atlanta on Monday.

Harold and Jerry drove to the Golf Hall of Fame Museum in St. Augustine, Florida.

Day 34: March 19, 2023

American Beach is historical. We met the curator/docent of A.L. Lewis Museum. She gave a very personal tour as she is the niece of MaVynee Oshun Betsch, "The Beach Lady." The docent shared her family connection to this beach and the importance of its place in our history. The Beach Lady almost single-handedly kept this beach for African Americans, even as resorts for the wealthy were being built around American Beach.

Day 35: March 20, 2023

We are packing up here on Cullen Court in Jacksonville and heading to Atlanta. I pray this visit in the ATL goes well. Harrison, our youngest, is meeting us there to spend his spring break with us. We need to have fruitful conversations with him to help shape our summer and fall plans and see how he fits into them. Cheri is so excited for us to come. I pray for traveling grace—it will be a long drive day.

Jacksonville's host was Jerry, Harold's dear friend from their early days in San Diego. He and his lovely wife, Linda, retired there after many years in Connecticut. Harold and Jerry were in the same class, graduating from Lincoln High together. They were in each other's weddings, and we have visited Jerry and Linda at each of their locations as they moved around the United States for Jerry's career. We watched each other's children grow up, and we recently received an invite for their son's wedding in Baltimore. Yay! Another place to travel to and explore.

Jerry and Linda's home is spectacular! It is a very large, two-story building with an elevator and a pool. They live on hole five of their country club golf course. They have done well and are now both retired and enjoy traveling. Jerry can literally pull his golf cart out from the garage, drive around the house, and be on the golf course. Harold was in heaven! He could live there: a gorgeous home with a pool right on the golf course, tastefully decorated for the two of them, yet able to host several family members or friends at once. They are also building a tri-level beach home at American Beach, Florida. We would love to visit here again, as well as visit the beach house once it's completed. It was very relaxing, in a beautiful and peaceful setting.

Jerry and Linda learned of American Beach and like to share it with all their visitors. Back in the 1930s, American Beach was one of the few places Blacks could feel safe while enjoying the beach. In 1935, it was the first beach in Florida to welcome African American guests overnight. Today, a group of African Americans are trying to keep the historical site preserved for African Americans despite large corporations trying to muscle their way into this beautiful oceanfront area. Our hosts are doing their part as they were able to purchase a lot and are constructing a beach home that will be kept in their family.

Reflections

Dig up your past dreams—look at that old vision board again! What have you always wanted to do if money wasn't the obstacle? Harold and I wanted to travel first in the United States then abroad. I have other interests to explore once we are settled into our new home.

Jerry and Linda are taking piano lessons, Jerry to learn the instrument and Linda to improve her skills. Is that your dream? To learn something new like an instrument, language, or other hobby?

They also shared that they keep their own schedule and maintain their own interests. In their retirement, Jerry and Linda have breakfast and dinner together. During the day they continue their separate activities and each are heavily involved in volunteering their time with several organizations.

My heart is full. God is so good. He loved us through our friends and family throughout this trip. I felt at peace with Jerry and Linda. We were very fortunate to have had such amazing hosts. We had five-star accommodations all the way. It's rare to find really good friends, but when the spouses get along also, now that's a bonus! We would like to visit with them more often and travel together, and we aim to make this happen since all of us are retired now.

———————

"Two can accomplish more than twice as much as one, for the results can be much better. If one falls, the other pulls him up; but if a man falls when he is alone, he's in trouble."

Ecclesiastes 4:9-10 (TLB)

10

Gorgeous Georgia

DAY 36: MARCH 21, 2023

Unable to sleep well last night—I was wide-eyed until about 5 a.m. Woke up at 9 a.m. It was a tough drive—a five-hour drive took us seven hours. Harold did well until he tried to hold my hand and swerved. It scared us both. We were able to visit Harold's friends, Ronald and Dwight, while waiting for Harrison's flight. They both live close to the airport. We got Harrison from the airport and stopped to grab some food. Arrived at Marcus' at about 10 p.m. It was challenging to find the right way to get onto the unfamiliar property in the darkness.

Day 37: March 22, 2023

We visited the Martin Luther King Center, then went to Morehouse/Clark Atlanta campus. While wandering around campus, we happened to run into Dylan and TJ. TJ was on his way to baseball practice.

Day 38: March 23, 2023

We are here alone; Harold and I seem distant. I don't know why I feel disconnected right now. We got some space since Harold was hanging out with Marcus and I was with Cheri.

Day 44: March 29, 2023

Last day in the ATL and it is time to go. We do like it here; I could live here. We've had great times with numerous friends and family. We have hit the wall, though. Harold and I have been together too much. We had a huge blowout yesterday and are still not *speaking. This may be a first since his stroke. From here, it's on to Ohio. It's been six weeks on the road. Some space between Harold and I would be nice.*

I am learning what I like and want. Also important is what I don't like or want. Harrison spent his spring break here. It was okay, but we continued to clash. Today Cheri and I had a long walk and talk. I was able to take a bath in her huge tub while she went to the dentist.

The drive from Jacksonville to Atlanta was stunning! Traveling north, while the interstate was beautifully tree lined, it was also sprinkled with sightings of the Confederate flag. This was "the South," and we had been warned. We had already passed by numerous Buc-ee's, especially through Texas. I recalled a news story about this larger-than-life establishment, so we had to experience it for ourselves. When it was time to gas up and take a break, we followed the signs to the nearest one. I wanted to see what all the hype was about.

The signs led us to a Buc-ee's in Georgia, and we discovered it is so much more than a truck stop—it was an incredible sight! Driving in, there were at least one hundred gas pumps in front of a huge one-story building, surrounded by ample parking. Outside the building were stacks of pallets of water and charcoal and a wide selection of barbecue grills lined up for sale. The look on our faces was probably priceless.

Entering the building, my immediate thought was that it was a combination of a Walmart, 7-Eleven, and truck stop all in one; it was known as a "travel center." The employees were warm and friendly and shouted out "welcome to Buc-ee's" as each group of customers entered. Buc-ee's offered a wide variety of food counters from a chef slicing roast beef and a counter showcasing at least twenty varieties of beef jerky to a few nuts and fudge counters. On the other side of the store were household items, clothing, and all sorts of local and Buc-ee's souvenirs. The store was full of people bustling about, with the line for the restroom spilling out into the beverage and coffee bar area. We walked around in amazement, trying to find our favorite snacks. As we left, we already looked forward to another chance to visit Buc-ee's.

While in Georgia, we split our time between two host families: Harold's brother Marcus and our dear friend Cheri whom I met at work. She was a pharmaceutical representative selling infant formula to Kaiser. We hit it off from the start, our spirits meshed. Cheri was the matron of honor in our wedding and I was in the delivery room with her first born.

Marcus moved away from Southern California many years ago. He encouraged his family members to join him in the Atlanta area, citing its beauty and lower cost of living. Cheri also moved away from Southern California about thirty years ago to be closer to her family in North Carolina and for job opportunities for her and her husband. Neither family has regretted leaving the coveted California.

Our son Harrison's spring break fell while we planned to be in Atlanta. This was his freshman year of college at University of Colorado, Denver. We continued to see God's hand guide and direct our trip. The timing again was perfect to allow him to fly in for a week, and we were happy to see him and hear all about his first semester away. He had several friends who were in Atlanta for college, including TJ and Dylan who were from Los Angeles and attended Morehouse.

As it turned out, in trying to catch up with another one of my former patients, Ellie, she suggested we meet her at Morehouse's baseball game as her friend was on the Clark Atlanta team. We thought that was a great idea as we were able to catch a game and watch TJ play: Morehouse versus Clark Atlanta, a school rivalry. TJ's mom happened to be in town and at the game. We had a chance to catch up with her. Jeff, another classmate of Harrison's, was also at the game. I was also able to visit with Ellie and a family friend from way back in the day, Cordie, who was able to meet us at that same game. He had been a part of our camping family. We met his family when I was about five years old and share many camping memories together. We had a nice visit with everyone while enjoying another college baseball game. It was awesome to see so many people from different parts of our lives meet up in one place. Now that's living our best lives! Back on Morehouse's campus, we briefly visited Raman. He, too, is a former patient of mine and high school classmate of Harrison's.

After the game, we met with more friends from Los Angeles for dinner at BarTaco by Inman Park, near the Beltline. We had a nice visit with Matthew, a childhood friend, and his wife Nicole, as well as with Tamiko, my teammate from high school. Inman Park is a hip area of Atlanta, crowded with young people, especially on a beautiful spring day. We were able to see a bit of the Beltline, packed with walkers, bikers, folks on scooters, and others simply laying out enjoying the great weather.

Tamiko, tired of life in Los Angeles, moved to Atlanta in 1992 after the riots that resulted from the Rodney King verdicts. She stayed for peace of mind and has not looked back. Matthew had been commuting from Los Angeles to Atlanta for work. When Nicole came for an extended visit, she enjoyed the environment so much that it made them weigh the benefits of living in each place. They settled in Peachtree City and continue to enjoy their decision.

Before we set out on this adventure, I had thought to myself that by the time we got to Atlanta, Harold and I would need some space apart. Atlanta seemed like the halfway point in terms of time if not mileage. We knew that being with one person, in the confining quarters of a car, venturing into the unknown was going to be challenging. Our relationship has been evolving since the stroke. I knew there would be challenges, and we have worked to maintain a healthy relationship. By Atlanta, after six weeks together full time, we were both ready for some space. He was able to be with his brother and I spent time with Cheri. Everyone needs some time apart; it's good for any relationship. Individuals need to have their own interests and hobbies. Harold enjoyed golfing a few times while I hung out with Cheri and her family. Ellie, her daughter, runs a dance studio and it was dance competition season. What a treat it was to witness my first dance competition. It was a wild scene with all the moving parts, coordinating the various teams into position and on stage for their routine.

A few days later, I was also able to celebrate her husband Jaime's birthday with them. As the party wrapped up and I was loading up my car, it started sprinkling. Not five minutes down the road, the heavens opened up and poured sheets of rain. It was one of those Atlanta thunderstorms I had heard about, one that looked like it might drive me off the road! Frequent loud claps of thunder mixed with darting lightning and howling wind seemed to come out of nowhere. The rain came down in sheets, and seemed to be hitting my car sideways. Windshield wipers were on the fastest setting but still not able to keep my view clear. I called Harold, but he did not answer. I called Cheri back who suggested I pull over to allow the storm to pass. I didn't want to stop, so I slowly pushed on, making headway on this forty-minute drive. Remembering I had shared my location with Harrison, Cheri stayed on the phone with me while Jaime called Harrison to alert him of my situation so he could follow my location until I made it back safely. She stayed on the phone with me, keeping me calm. The storm let up slightly and I made it back to Marcus'. I pulled in and took a breath. I was thankful to have made it back, rattled but safe. Harold had been waiting for me in the driveway, his phone inside, left charging. While I have driven in rain, wind, snow, ice, and hail, I have never driven in weather that made me tremble in fear.

The next day, Cheri drove us three hours to the Legacy Museum in Montgomery, Alabama. Wow! This is a "must see" for everyone. Bryan Stevenson and the Equal Justice Initiative did not hold back in reviewing and presenting 400 years of racial injustice. The information was presented thoughtfully and strategically. Some scenes and exhibits were so graphic that at times I felt physically ill. We took our time through the museum, yet likely missed so much.

Another former patient, Ajana, a student at Tuskegee, was able to join us for lunch at the on-site café and the second half of our tour. I'm glad I was able to spend some time with Ajana. She's doing big things on Tuskegee's campus. She was the fifth former patient of mine I was able to connect with. That was heartwarming both ways.

After lunch, we took the shuttle to the National Memorial for Peace and Justice and walked under all those beams, each one representing one or more lynchings of United States citizens. The rows and rows of beams gave me an eerie sensation. More than 800 steel columns represent the nearly 4,400 Black Americans terrorized by this inhumane treatment.

To top off our day, Cheri suggested we stop by Jonesboro, where the cousins live whose daughter recently passed away. Although it was a bit out of our way and we already had a long, emotional day at the museums, I was grateful we stopped by to pay our respects to the parents of the sixteen-year-old who had died about five weeks prior.

Some family members from New Orleans were still there, and it was good to fellowship with extended family and friends. It's always difficult when a child dies, but when God chooses a living angel, one of His best girls, those who are left behind struggle to put the pieces back together. It's a puzzle that will forever have a missing piece.

Harrison's spring break came to an end. We dropped him off at the airport and continued east. Harold's friend from San Diego now living in Conyers, Georgia, had invited us for breakfast. Donald and his wife must've woken up before dawn to prepare this amazing breakfast. Food covered the entire kitchen island and all the countertops. They had everything one could ask for: waffles and eggs, bacon and pastries, grits and croissants and more, just for the four of us. We felt their love through the food.

After ten days in the greater Atlanta area, it was time to hit the road again. We packed the car the night before, and were ready to roll in the morning.

Reflections

We were able to do a lot and see even more in the Atlanta area since we have a nice collection of friends and family from Southern California who have made Georgia their home. They all shared their stories of how they got there. I can see myself living in Georgia. I enjoyed the tree-filled landscapes, the variety in weather, and being closer to the east coast where there is so much more to explore.

Someone recently shared with me the idea that you shouldn't be born and raised and live and die in the same location. Begin to think about areas you might want to explore. If you can save some money, start now and be consistent. Make it a regular and automatic deduction from your bank account.

We have always lived below our means, always conscious of saving resources. I can remember growing up in the seventies in California where conservation was a mantra. In our household, we had to turn lights off when leaving a room and turn water off while brushing our teeth. My frugal ways could've also come from our camping days where we had to use very little water to shower as well as to wash dishes. This carried over to money and a way of life for me. I was taught to save at least ten percent of my check, clip coupons, and look for the deal. Such a lifestyle has afforded me the ability to take an early retirement and not worry about our now "fixed income."

Again, I urge you to begin to think about ways to use less, spend less, and save more.

———

"The wise man saves for the future, but the foolish man spends whatever he gets."

Proverbs 21:20 (TLB)

We begin our journey.

Our loaded car.

*Dinner with Kym and Toni
in the Phoenix area.*

Good times in New Mexico.

Dinner with the Manleys in Fort Worth.
We picked up another friend!

All smiles with our Cypress, Texas hosts

Fun in the hot sun at LSU baseball game.

A quick stop with cousins near Mobile, Alabama.

Harold preparing for the golf course, Jacksonville, Florida.

Cheri and Jaime proved southern hospitality near Atlanta, Georgia.

Getting friendly with farm animals in Jeromesville, Ohio.

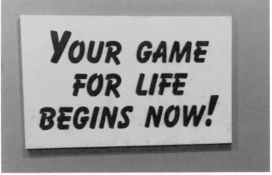

This Pro Football Hall of Fame slogan is always relevant.

Easter Sunday with Pastor Luke at Good News in the Neighborhood, outside Chicago, Illinois.

The Architectural River Boat Tour, Chicago, Illinois.

At the spring football game. The coldest day of our trip. GO BUFFS!

Night of jazz with friends.

11

Small Town Experience In Ohio

DAY 47: APRIL 1, 2023

We had bad weather from Kentucky to here. It was raining heavily, visibility was poor.

We arrived in Jeromesville, Ohio. It was another long driving day—354 miles took us about eight hours. Harold was able to help drive about thirty minutes, about thirty miles, from one rest stop to the next. We had several stops, including lunch at Kroger's where we tried to wait out the storm. It was pouring rain with low visibility at times. It was bad but not as

scary as driving back to Marcus' after Jaime's birth-
day.

Day 51: April 5, 2023

We have been with Patty in Jeromesville, Ohio, for the past five days. Patty has fed us well. We have gone out to her parents a few times. They live at the small local airport, but are currently in Florida at their winter location. We've watched the NCAA basketball playoffs, skydivers fall from the sky, and we roller skated on the runway. My car was serviced in Canton while we enjoyed the Pro Football Hall of Fame.

We were fortunate to have a personal tour of the Hall. We took our time, taking in all the history of the game.

We visited a farm, getting up close and personal with cows and horses. We have one more day here. We saw the movie Air *today and will visit Amish culture tomorrow. Next stop: Chicago.*

From Atlanta to our next host in Ohio was again a bit too long to drive in one day. We took Interstate 75 north to just outside of Lexington, Kentucky, and spent the night in a lovely Airbnb.

The next morning, we had some weather. It was raining, and visibility was limited due to the heavy rain. We reached out to Patty with frequent updates of our progress. We took it slow, continuing northeast on Interstate 75 until we transitioned to Interstate 71 outside of Cincinnati before arriving in Jeromesville, Ohio.

Patty, our next hostess, took a few days off of work to be with us. We knew Patty from our youth football days when our kids played in the El Segundo league. She and I became close over the years while walking around the track and neighborhood during the boys' practices.

That routine continued when we transferred to a different league. Our relationship endured even after she moved back to Ohio. She and I have remained in touch, continuing to share the joys and pains of life.

Her hometown is small and everyone knows each other, and most everyone is White. No matter, we were warmly welcomed at her church, the farm, and everywhere else she took us. Olivia, her daughter, was away at college. We enjoyed her home, hospitality, and Harlo, the family dog.

Patty lives in a rural area of Ohio that is dotted with small, family-run farms. She arranged for us to have a personal tour of one. The father-daughter duo showed off their cattle and horses and talked about a day in their life on the farm. The father would soon retire from his firefighter career to manage his farm full time. The daughter had regular chores to keep the farm functioning and offset the upkeep of her personal horse.

The next day, Patty and I went on a hike in Mohican State Park, while Harold golfed with one of her friends. We all enjoyed getting physical in the beautiful outdoors. It was a warm sunny day as we walked along Clear Fork Mohican River listening to Mother Nature in the leaves and streams.

We packed a lot into our few days together. Harold made reservations for the Pro Football Hall of Fame for the following day. This was on our "must see" list since we were in proximity. It has changed dramatically from the first time Harold and I visited twenty years ago.

The reception starts on Highway 77 with beautiful artwork on overpasses that welcome visitors in, and as we arrived, we were greeted with smiles and a warm welcome.

We met our guide for the day and started our personal tour. We learned the history of the sport as we walked through the various exhibits. To see all the busts on display was a little overwhelming. We all were on the hunt for our favorite players so we could then pose for a picture with them.

These museums are wise to have a café inside them. We broke for a bite to eat, then continued on to complete the tour.

Reflections

While Patty isn't retired, her parents are. We didn't get a chance to meet them as they are snow birds. They drive their RV to the warmth of Florida to escape the harsh winter of Ohio. Splitting time between more than one location is something many people do and an idea we toy with as well. It's retirement! You can do whatever you want to do. Let the dreams begin!

Remember to start saving for your dreams. Consider a fiduciary or fee-only financial advisor. This is one that won't push a certain product to benefit themselves or the company they represent. They should only have your best interest in mind, taking into account such things as your risk tolerance and how much time remains before your retirement date.

Up to this point, we stayed with several families of different races. One way for different cultures to get along is by spending time with them. Traveling to different destinations, having an open mind, being curious, and having a desire to build bridges can be a way to heal cultural wounds. Through our brief travels and staying with various families, it is evident that various cultures have more in common; we are more alike than not.

"The alien living with you must be treated as one of your native-born. Love him as yourself, for you were aliens in Egypt. I am the Lord your God."

Leviticus 19:34 (NIV)

12

Springtime In Chicago

DAY 56: APRIL 10, 2023

We arrived in Chicago last Friday, April 7th, Good Friday. Lots of activity with the kids and Bran. We rested Saturday which has been our pattern to do the first day at the new location. Although the drive wasn't too bad since Harold asked Patty to drive part of the way. She wanted us to see her daughter, Olivia, and to meet Adrian, Olivia's boyfriend. They both are away at college about ninety minutes from Jeromesville. That cut my drive time down.

On Easter morning, we drove almost an hour to Pastor Luke's church, Good News in the Neighborhood, located in Palatine. We surprised him good! It was a wonderful service; Pastor Luke delivered a great word using Jenga blocks.

Gab prepared a delicious veggie pie dinner served with red beans and rice. She made hot cross buns to honor Matt and his native England where hot cross buns are a staple. I met up with Becky, whom I had been trying to reach for years. She took me out for tapas and cocktails. Harold got a haircut, not such a good one. We miss Cameron, his fantastic barber back home. Harold also got to hang out with Michael, an associate from college.

DAY 58: APRIL 12, 2023

We listened to jazz at the Bronzeville Winery right here in the neighborhood. Becky is a member of Chicago Jazz and was able to secure tickets and seats for the show. Tuesday, Harold and I walked along the lake, then ran some errands. We will make dinner tonight and allow Matt and Gabby to have a date night. We experienced the Architectural River Tour and deep dish pizza. Cousin Ray had taken us to Malnati's. Tuesday, he took us to Uncle Julio's and Harold's Chicken. We visited his high-rise apartment, toured the pool and spa areas, and enjoyed his great view of Lake Michigan. Tomorrow we will chill, do laundry, pack up, eat up the leftovers, and be ready to hit the road Friday.

Chicago is our most northern destination. After leaving Patty, Olivia, and Adrian, we took Interstate 80/90 west through Indiana. It was a pleasant drive passing by small towns and farming communities.

Our host point person there was Gabby. She is the daughter of Gary and Marilyn, whose home we stayed at in Arlington, Texas earlier in our trip. They were our absent hosts, as they had been in Chicago helping with their grandchildren. Gabby lives in the Hyde Park area of Chicago with Matt, her husband, and their two young children, Jude, a bright two-year-old, just shy of three, and Vivienne, an adventurous eighteen-month-old, and the family dog Bran. Prior to this trip, I had not spent much time with Gabby and her family, and she hadn't known Harold previously. But she and Matt welcomed us and made us feel right at home.

We also got a chance to spend time with Jude and Vivienne. Vivienne is special to me because she was named with my mother Vivienne in mind. They spell it the same, which is not the most common spelling. Wow! She's adorable but quite the "pistol," just like her namesake. Being a toddler, it's her job to want everything her way; toddlers are learning there is a world outside of them. I had initially met her when she was a newborn, and boy did she cry when I attempted to hold her. Me! The pediatric healthcare provider. I always prided myself in being a sort of "baby whisperer," able to quiet even the fussiest of babies. Vivi, as she is called, wasn't having any of it. Way to humble me, Vivienne! Now a toddler, she was slow to warm up, but by the end of our visit, we were buddies.

This young family has a lovely brownstone home in a historic district of Chicago close to Lake Michigan, which was an ideal location. They weren't far from Harold's college associate, Michael, or his cousin Ray.

Ray has lived in Chicago for many years. He is from Los Angeles, but moved away to attend college in Texas. From there, he migrated to Chicago. Ray showed us around downtown, pointed out where historic Cabrini Green once stood, and took us to some of his favorite local eateries until we couldn't eat anymore. We appreciated Ray taking time for us.

Packed in this week was the Architectural River Tour. It was phenomenal—so glad we didn't miss that. We learned so much about the history of Chicago as well as reasons behind why the buildings are constructed in such a unique way. The buildings along the Chicago River actually tell a fascinating story.

While in Chicago, we also planned to surprise a former pastor from our church. Pastor Luke had been on staff there for several years before going back to his hometown of Chicago. We enjoyed learning from him at Wednesday night services. He was only the second Caucasian pastor we've had at Faithful Central Bible Church. He was always received warmly and brought his unique perspective to his teachings, sharing personal stories about raising his four children. He and his wife Kristen have now planted a multicultural church in the city of Palatine, a suburb of Chicago. Easter service is usually crowded at most churches, so we allowed plenty of time to drive to the location, find a good parking spot, and get a great seat. Little did I know, Pastor Luke had been following our trip on Facebook. He was extremely shocked when he saw us standing in the reception area waiting to enter the sanctuary. His reaction was priceless!

Next I aimed to connect with another old friend. I met Becky at University of Colorado, Boulder (CU), and we grew close throughout our college days. I had traveled with her to Chicago twice and she came out to Los Angeles to assist with and attend our wedding. Over the years and distance, we lost contact. I found some numbers for her in my old phone book, none of which worked. While in Chicago, I reached out to a mutual friend also from CU, hoping to get an updated phone number for Becky. That worked! I'm grateful to have reconnected with Becky.

Reflections

Each city and state definitely had its own personality and culture. I'm very grateful to have been able to do such an excursion to see it for myself. Thankfully we had no issues with anyone or anything.

I've always believed one can learn something from anybody if you are open and curious to learn. Living with this family for a week, I witnessed cooperation among all of them, including Bran, the dog. It was also refreshing to see the sibling dynamic at this tender age. Jude is the loving, intelligent older brother while Vivi is the curious, younger sibling who loves being with her family. Oh to be a kid again. Adulting isn't always pleasant.

———————

"Let the children alone, don't prevent them from coming to me. God's kingdom is made up of people like these."

Matthew 19:14 (MSG)

13

Middle America

DAY 63: APRIL 17, 2023

We left Chicago as planned. Made it to Boudurant, Iowa, just east of Des Moines. We had a lovely Airbnb on a small lake. It seemed like a new remodel with great light fixtures and a comfy bed. We had our deep dish leftovers with veggies. We then left for our next pit stop, Lexington, Nebraska. This time we were at Holiday Inn Express. We both spent time in the fitness center, which is why Harold wanted a hotel tonight, for the gym. While on the tread-mill, I watched an Adam Sandler movie already in progress. Intrigued, I had to google it. It was Hidden Gems. *I couldn't sleep that night so I caught another movie halfway through titled* Men. *Both movies caught my attention; I made a note to see both in their entirety at some point. We ate the hotel hot breakfast buffet. It was decent; it got us on our way to Denver. Since I didn't sleep well, the drive was particularly tough. Harold was able to drive twice, but I still needed to pull into a rest area in Wiggins, Colorado. I took a power nap.*

What made the drive more challenging was trying to bring up a sensitive topic. I thought I had handled it safely and respectfully, but it backfired. That was weird; we aren't talking today.

We made it to Denver. Went straight to campus to pick up Harrison. Even though we gave him an ETA, we had to wait for him… again! No one really talked, even at dinner.

Harrison was on his phone with, I think, legitimate stuff like school, but since no one was talking, I didn't see the need to ask him to get off. We headed to Boulder after dropping him back to his dorm.

I took a nice shower; it was great, hot water with a nice flow. I slept well. Today we have just been relaxing. We walked a bit earlier and spent time in the backyard clearing off two chairs and a table, setting up the recliner, and turning on the waterfall in the pond.

Chicago to Denver was about a thousand miles, so we did two overnights, one in an Airbnb and the other in a hotel on our way to our next destination. We drove west on Interstate 80, taking us through mostly flat, farming communities. Once we arrived at our stop for the night, a beautiful Airbnb outside Des Moines, Iowa, I enjoyed some happy hour treats outside while taking in the view of the lake at sunset. We had a good night's rest after dinner. In the morning, we packed up the car with the few things we brought in and headed to our next pit stop in Lexington, Nebraska.

We were well into the day's drive when I asked Harold if he remembered packing my pillow. I didn't remember seeing it or bringing it out to the car. I had tossed and turned so much, trying to get to sleep, the pillow must've buried itself between the sheets. I continued to drive while Harold left a message for the hotel manager. A couple of days passed before they were able to connect. The pillow was found and the manager stated he would mail it to us. Disaster averted!

We continued traveling west on Interstate 80 where we saw more flat lands, more farming communities, and sprinkles of rain. As we settled into our hotel room, I used my phone to search for a nearby restaurant for dinner. We agreed on the local Mexican restaurant I found online. The front desk staff assured us that it was good and within walking distance. It was dusk when we started out. We were the only pedestrians out, but we needed some exercise after so much sitting. We could see the restaurant in the distance, but it was farther than we thought. Finally arriving, we felt we were in for a treat since the staff spoke very little English. The food was amazing! We were so full I considered getting an Uber ride back. That would have been silly. But by then it was dark, the wind was howling, and we were chilly with only light jackets on. We headed out on foot, as drivers passed by probably wondering why the heck we were out there. We laughed at ourselves all the way back. It helped to keep us warm.

Reflections

Springtime in Chicago was absolutely beautiful! As we drove through middle America, our thoughts of where we wanted to live continued to take shape. We like experiencing different types of weather; people think we are odd to want to leave sunny California. But after spending my college years in Colorado, I looked forward to experiencing all four seasons. Los Angeles has subtle changes in weather. Also, we like to spend time outdoors, enjoying beautiful scenery. We both like to walk, I like water activities, and Harold enjoys golf. A smaller home would be okay as it's just the two of us now. However, we do want a home with ample room to welcome our sons, family, and friends, or any travelers we can repay.

If you're married, you may be able to relate to periods of time when the communication doesn't flow. This could be for a variety of reasons. Over our thirty-three-year relationship, we have had various types of counseling and small group experiences to assist with our relationship, but sometimes we just get stuck and stubborn. The single greatest tip I learned, albeit late in the game, was to respect my husband. It sounds so simple, but men need unconditional respect. It's in the Bible—check out Ephesians 5:33 where it says, "However, each one of you also must love his wife as he loves himself, and the wife must respect her husband." Men feel loved when they feel respected. While men and women are very different, the couple can thrive when the wife feels loved and the husband feels respected.

Realizing that there will be challenging times in any relationship may help keep couples in it for the long haul. Just knowing that there will be troubling situations can help you expect them and learn to work through them. These days I often reflect on the marriage vow "in sickness and in health."

Too often, people don't keep their vows and are ready to jump ship at the slightest inconvenience. We are a living example that if you hang in there long enough, your efforts will pay off.

———————

"Let us not be weary in doing good, for at the proper time we will reap a harvest, if we do not give up."

Galatians 6:9 (NIV)

14

Colorado Connections

DAY 64: APRIL 18, 2023

It's Tuesday. Harold and I joke but it's true, we can't keep up with what day it is. That's retired life! But we have plans to be with Harrison today and Thursday. We had breakfast, then ran a few errands on the way to his campus. I texted Harrison along the way with our ETA. We updated him and reached out again with no response to any of my texts. I found that odd since he knew we had plans today. But our relationship is still a work… in progress. Then I remembered he shares his location with me. I checked his location.

He was at a hospital. Frantic but trying to stay calm, I zoomed in on the location—he was in the emergency room! My heart sank. Trying to rationalize, I said to myself, "His phone is there. Did someone take his phone?! Why is his phone at the hospital?" Trying to breathe and pray, we arrived safely at the emergency room. We park and go through security, which was akin to TSA at the airport. These agents were very thorough. The lady in front of us had a vape pen taken away. Guards were discussing whether it was tobacco or THC. I guess it didn't matter, they confiscated it anyway.

By now my heart was pounding. We got to the clerk and I couldn't speak. She asked how she could help us and words would not come out of my mouth. Only tears came down my cheeks. Harold took over the conversation and stated why we were there. She told us where Harrison was. I was surprised they gave us any information at all. He was nineteen years old, and in California, over eighteen, they do not have to disclose health information without the patient's permission. After a short wait and going through another metal detector, we got to his room. There he lay face down asleep. I touch his waist, calling his name. He is groggy and doesn't know what happened. The nurse came in, introduced herself and advised us to wait for the doctor. After some time of being there, the doctor came in. We learn he was with friends overnight and around 8 a.m. he had a medical emergency, was disoriented and combative. They responded appropriately and called 911. Paramedics transported him here to the emergency room. The doctor said that Harrison had an adverse reaction, that he needed to sleep it off, and proceeded to discharge him. Praise the Lord!

I'm so thankful we were in town and that Harrison had shared his location. Thankful that he'll be okay. Thankful that the police didn't come. He simply had to sleep it off. And that he did. We arrived back in Boulder that afternoon. He slept the rest of that day and night and was able to make it to class the next day.

DAY 65: APRIL 19, 2023

Yesterday Harrison awoke about 10 a.m. I wanted to get to Denver asap to pick up his ring that was left at the friend's during his medical emergency.

Harrison was better, more alert and coherent. We arrived and met Niko, and thanked him for helping Harrison the day before. Harrison collected all of his belongings and we continued on to campus.

As we get closer to campus, we notice parking signs for a Colorado Rockies baseball game. We dropped Harrison off at school, but weren't sure what we were going to do for the rest of the day. We didn't have any plans. We went for a much-needed car wash. While at the car wash, I got on the internet to see about tickets for the Rockies game. For this midweek, midday game, they advertised nine dollar tickets. Harold said, "Yes, let's go." We drove over to Coors Field, found parking right across the street for forty dollars. That was okay because the tickets were so inexpensive. When Harold went to buy the nine-dollar tickets, the agent offered one-dollar tickets. How cool is that? We sat way up top where it was a bit chilly. I didn't have the right jacket on and I left my glasses in the car. It was a cloudy day. The sun peeked out only about two to three times. We left after the third inning, when the score was already nine to nothing. We walked over to D'Corazon Restaurant and enjoyed our lunch before heading back to Boulder. We stopped at Crumbl Cookies, Target, and King Soopers. I roasted veggies to go along with our dinner and dessert.

DAY 67: APRIL 21, 2023

I slept well and got up on my own to watch Good Morning America. *We headed out to Costco, and on the way we stopped at Davidson Mesa Open Space, walked about twenty minutes, then continued to Costco. We gassed up and went in to get my glasses adjusted and a few items. On the way back, we stopped at the lake across from Davidson. All of these stops outdoors are a trial run for tomorrow in terms of clothing needed to stay warm at the spring football game. Chris and Rob had us over for a delicious shrimp taco feast. I babysat for their girls on occasion during my eight-year stay in Boulder.*

Day 69: April 23, 2023

Yesterday was Black and Gold Day (CU football spring game) and it snowed! It snowed overnight, leaving a thin layer on Wendy's lawn. When we got to the stadium, the bleachers had about two inches of snow on them. Jim cleared it away and we sat close together in an attempt to stay warm. It was the coldest day so far, and we had to be out in it. It continued to snow lightly on and off during the game. Folsom Field was packed, the game was sold out! Coach Prime and the team did not disappoint, but we left at halftime. It was SO cold! We heated up a frozen pizza to go with a salad and then joined the Champion Couples Gathering (couples ministry from church) on Zoom.

Today we had church service. We bless God for Pastor JP. He took over at Faithful Central and is doing an amazing job. Went to visit Vivian, Kym's mother (she was our host in Arizona), where we watched a bit of the New York Knicks versus Cleveland Cavs game with her. I had a cup of coffee and a slice of cake, not wanting to disappoint Ms. Vivian. After that, we went to campus to help Harrison orga-nize his move out of the dorm. We got to his room but he didn't seem quite ready for us so we set-tled in to wait. We allotted a bit over two hours. We packed a bin of winter items and things he wouldn't need with only a few weeks left of school. We had limited time as I had salmon thawing in a cold bag in the car. We are hosting dinner at Zan and Jim's.

DAY 73: APRIL 27, 2023

Yesterday we toured campus in Boulder. Harold wanted to reenact a photo of me walking out of Norlin Library that Zan found many years ago. She mailed it to me shortly after I started working at Kaiser, and it hung in my office for years, remind-ing me of my years on that campus. We took a few pictures at the library and the stadium. We drove up Mapleton looking out for Lyons Lair hiking trail, a recommendation from Chris. We did our twen-ty-minute walk, then stopped at Safeway looking for some CU swag. Went back to Wendy's to visit with her. She's home from Vietnam. We rested, had lunch, then got ready for jazz at Nissi's with Jim, Zan, and Charlotte. Nelson Rangell played the sax and flute.

DAY 74: APRIL 28, 2023

I seem to be a day behind. Yesterday, Harold played golf with Jim and two of his buddies, Kenneth and Darrell. While they golfed, Zan and I hung out. I truly had a home spa day. Zan had a tray of nail care items laid out, complete with a variety of polish colors. I sat outdoors doing my nails, later having lunch before soaking in their hot tub. I painted my nails while Zan and I talked some more. The icing on the cake was the massage chair. Ahh, this was a real deal massage chair! When the golfers returned, we jetted out to get back to Wendy. She prepared shrimp pasta for dinner, complete with appetizers, cocktails, and dessert.

Today we may go for a walk, then drive around. Wendy would like us to move here. It's expensive, though, almost like California. We have dinner reservations tonight with Dave and Lyn.

Day 76: April 30, 2023

Road day. Nice pit stop in Glenwood Hot Springs. We left at about 9 a.m. Arrived at Glenwood Hot Springs about noon. What a great place for a rest. The hot springs were awesome, and I am so glad we took our time and did not rush to get to our motel room for the night. The Budget Inn, Green River, Utah, was a new low of motels for us.

We continued west on Interstate 80 until it intersected with Interstate 76. That took us all the way to Denver, Colorado, to have dinner with Harrison before heading up to Boulder, our host home for the next two weeks. Wendy was our host in Boulder. I met Wendy and her family while I was an undergraduate student at the University of Colorado, Boulder. We met at the local gym where she exercised often and I worked in the children's nursery.

This led to me babysitting her two children, and other kids from the gym, at their home as needed.

We remained friends; she and her family have stayed with us a few times in Los Angeles and I often stay at her home when visiting Colorado. During this visit, she was on vacation in Vietnam, but allowed us to have her home to ourselves for the first several days. She had given me clear instructions on everything.

The weather in Colorado can be quite unpredictable and with wide temperature fluctuations. It was expected to get cooler, but as it got closer to game day, snow was in the forecast. I didn't want to believe it, but when we woke up Saturday morning, surely there was a layer of snow covering the ground.

Now we really had all types of weather on this trip! We had unseasonably warm weather for most of the trip. We've had rain, thunderstorms, and now snow. Colorado is known for its varying weather that can change dramatically all in one day. But leave it to Colorado to have snow on April 22nd!

Jim joined us for the football game. He and Zan have been wonderful contacts over the years. I met Zan in the early eighties while I was an undergraduate student at CU. I have such great friends in Colorado, which is one reason I return there when I can. Of course the beauty of the state, its seasons, the majestic Flatirons of Boulder, and the numerous outdoor options are a continual draw for me to return to the state in which I became an adult. I can always count on Zan for great company, an awesome meal, and authentic hospitality.

Another contact we like to visit in Colorado is Dave, who was my classmate and Master's thesis partner in the physician assistant program. We have kept in touch since our graduation in 1989. He also worked for Kaiser Permanente but in Denver. We often swapped work stories and made time for each other on my visits to Colorado. I like hanging out with Dave and Lyn because they demonstrate what a loving and successful marriage looks like.

One highlight of this trip to Colorado was receiving my pillow! The manager from the Nebraska Holiday

Inn was kind enough to mail it to us at Wendy's at no charge. This pillow is like a favorite stuffed animal. I find it helpful to have in order to sleep well ever since neck issues from computer use.

I was grateful the hotel staff kept their word and mailed my pillow. I appreciate it when people show kindness and integrity.

College in Colorado was the best! It was there that I was "on my own" and had to make all my decisions while getting through undergraduate and graduate school. Colorado experiences the four seasons and is known for its green spaces.

The amount of parks and trails is impressive, contributing to Colorado being one of the states with the lowest obesity rates. Colorado is on the short list of relocation possibilities.

Reflections

Retirement is for your enjoyment; it is your reward for putting those many years into your career pouring into others.

Take my friend Zan; she dove into her passion in retirement. She had dabbled in poetry for years, but it wasn't until she retired that she was able to devote adequate time to this gift and talent.

Since then she has become a bestselling poet with her own publications as well as contributing to several anthologies. She was my number one cheerleader for writing this book.

Or take my friend Wendy, who continued her exercise routine of hiking and aerial acrobatics after retiring. She volunteers with Make-A-Wish and tutors high school students in Spanish. Dave and Lyn also volunteer with their groups of interest and continue their exercise routine as well as travel internationally in between several runs to Texas.

In all of my different friend groups, they all continue to exercise, volunteer their time, and travel several times a year.

Retirement is your time, go after it!

"God has given each of us the ability to do certain things well."

Romans 12:6 (TLB)

15

Oh No! Last Stop
Las Vegas

DAY 78: MAY 2, 2023

Made it to Las Vegas yesterday at 4 p.m. Again, we didn't factor in the time zone change. Dwight and Letty have a beautiful home. I'm feeling sad about our trip coming to an end. Las Vegas has been lovely so far. Temperature is good, yesterday was in the eighties and windy. To hear Dwight talk about how great of a mentor Harold was to him... all I could think about was our boys.

We ate at Flower Child, good salmon with broccoli and snap peas.

DAY 79: MAY 3, 2023

Yesterday we lounged around resting from the drive. Harold golfed while I stayed back with the dogs, Sneaky and Simon. I stretched, did my dumbbells. I met Roni, Dwight's sister, for a walk as she shared about her cancer diagnosis, family stuff, her work, etc. I didn't know she felt such love for us.

We surprised Miles at his restaurant, had lunch as he waited on us.

Dwight and Letty took us to Bonefish Grill for dinner.

DAY 80: MAY 4, 2023

We got ready for our final leg, the drive to Los Angeles. I'm feeling sad that this awesome, wonderful adventure is coming to a close. We are grateful we were able to complete this feat unscathed. The only incident was minor—we sustained a cracked windshield heading out of Albuquerque.

We packed the car, said our goodbyes. In the morning, we will hop in the car and go.

Day 81: May 5, 2023

We got up to hit the road for LA. There's traffic, as usual, the closer we get to the city. We made it safely. We get to our Airbnb, thankful to have been able to travel across the United States, knowing that God's hand was on us, protecting and guiding our every move!

Our next host, Dwight, was one of Harold's mentees from the youth choir at church. Harold continued to keep tabs on his tenors as he was the adult mentor for the tenor section of the youth choir. He was there not only to keep order but also to be a role model for the teens. At the time, most of them lived nearby, which made it easy for him to check in on them periodically, even into their adulthood.

During our time in Las Vegas, we drove through a fifty-five-plus community. It was set up like a small town. I didn't care for the landscape in Vegas; the desert motif was not appealing to me. We know many people who have moved to Las Vegas, like Miles. He's the son of a dear friend from Los Angeles. Vegas is a quick four-hour jaunt from Los Angeles, depending on traffic. If we're going to move away, the next location must be attractive to all of our senses. We also want to continue with some international travel, and flying anywhere from the Las Vegas airport would require at least one stop to get to an international airport. These features will shape our decision to relocate.

On our last night there, we were able to visit with another member of the huge New Orleans family. We broke bread at Blaze Pizza. What a blessing to see Jolene and her daughter.

As we returned home, I updated our Facebook followers:

We made it back to Los Angeles!! To God be the glory; we were able to see His handiwork across our nation. We were able to feel His love through our 14 awesome host families and other friends and family that also fed and entertained us!! We had His protection for the 8,400 miles driving through 18 states! Thank you for your prayers, thank you for following along! We had a whole bunch of fun!!

Reflections

Be kind, and treat others the way you want to be treated. The old Golden Rule always applies. Who wants to be with anyone who is mean, grumpy, or rude? You are what you attract.

These families didn't have to take us into their home. They wanted to! You really get to know people when invited into their private settings. We had the opportunity to see how people live behind closed doors. That's relationship!

Be open to try new things. Take on a challenge. Remember, I didn't consider myself a long-distance driver. But here I am, having completed a cross-country road trip. I'm glad I didn't give into my feelings, that we didn't listen to the naysayers, and I'm proud of this accomplishment.

———————

"Do for others what you want them to do for you."

Matthew 7:12 (TLB)

16

The Finale

We rented a series of Airbnbs and spent the summer back home in the Los Angeles area. We needed furnished places since all of our home furnishings were in storage. It also served to fulfill my dream of living near the ocean since our first month was in Playa Vista, a planned community about a mile from the beach.

The next month was spent a bit south in Long Beach. Our apartment was right across the street from the bay. We enjoyed the beach life, and we were able to have our family join us for the Fourth of July celebration. We didn't have to travel anywhere for fireworks because the community of Bel-mont Shores had an awesome fireworks display. I am thankful for this beach experience, because I now know I wouldn't want to deal with sand per-manently. During the final month of summer, we returned to reality, back to our neighborhood in Los Angeles. We had medical appointments and other adult responsibilities to handle before our next ad-venture.

During mid-August 2023, we drove Harrison back to Colorado for his second year at CU Denver. Taking our time, we spent two nights again with Dwight and Letty in Las Vegas. Glenwood Springs, Col-orado, was so impressive as a rest stop that we spent a night there as well before arriving in Denver. We stayed in Denver for about a month because Airbnb fees were cheaper there than in Los Angeles. We also had a commitment in late September to be in New Mexico.

From Denver we drove back to Loree's in New Mex-ico. We were to house sit and care for her dog, Jill, while Loree took a long-overdue vacation. The timing was perfect because while there, we were able to enjoy the International Hot Air Balloon Fiesta, mostly from her backyard. It was incredible to see hundreds of hot air balloons take off, float around, and travel with the wind.

We enjoyed being outside with Jill. She was eleven years old and had already outlived her life expectancy. Unfortunately, while we were house sitting and caring for Jill, one day she simply stopped moving. I contacted Loree and she gave me instructions while she reached out to a mobile veterinarian. Sadly, Jill died the next day. We spent several more days there before departing for Los Angeles. Two or three days after we left, Loree had a serious medical issue requiring about a three-week hospitalization. After all of that, she wound up putting her house up for sale and moving to Colorado to live with her daughter until she could find her own place. I'm glad we were there for Loree and her family. Our families are forever bonded.

In October 2023, we participated in our church's group trip to Greece. About 150 of us followed the footsteps of Apostle Paul under the leadership of our dear Bishop Kenneth and Lady Tee Ulmer. Not only did it make Paul's letters of the Bible come to life, we also made some new fantastic relationships.

From there, Harold and I spent five days in Portugal, checking that country off our bucket list. We had a few tours in and around Lisbon. This country holds a lot of history and beautiful architecture.

After arriving home, we knew we had a decision to make: where would we settle now? From our travels through eighteen states, one location stood out to both of us. We landed in the greater Atlanta area as our place to retire. Georgia offers four spectacular seasons, and we look forward to watching the natural beauty of the area change with the time of year. It also boasts many lakes, rivers, and creeks, which can satisfy my love for water. The fact that we have numerous friends and family already there provides us with a sense of community. It also has an international airport and plenty to investigate on the East and Gulf Coasts. We plan to rent in a couple of areas, research different communities, and visit more fifty-five-plus communities before purchasing our next home.

Are you inspired now? Do you have some ideas on how to enjoy your life after work? Now get after it and explore. The world is bigger than your block!

———————

"But seek first His kingdom and His righteousness, and all these things will be given to you as well."

Matthew 6:33 (NIV)

17

Take Home Lessons

I want to leave you with the five most impactful lessons I learned through this experience.

Lesson #1: Have a plan, but be flexible.

We did the best we could mapping out a plan before we began our trip, but we also knew we'd need to be flexible along the way. For example, we originally wanted to go to Atlanta from Louisiana, but Harrison's spring break week and time constraints from our Florida hosts made it easy to pivot.

We also had Boston and Minnesota on our original route. Boston was deferred because we didn't want to feel rushed to get back west to Ohio. At our pace of about 300 miles a day, it was going to take too long to get that far north to Boston, then get to Ohio.

By that point, our hosts had timed us into their schedules. We didn't want to disrupt their lives too much. Also, I was intimidated at the thought of navigating the Eastern Seaboard with its numerous toll roads.

Minnesota was also removed since one of the hosts was going to be out of town. Again, it was going to take too long to get there and then down to Denver.

The original route may have been a bit too adventurous for our first extensive road trip. I'm glad we were able to shift when needed. That took the pressure off, and we were able to do what was comfortable.

Lesson #2: Retire as soon as you can.

This one I learned primarily from my father. He's now been retired longer than the years he served the City of Los Angeles. Then, the retirement age was fifty-five. Now, "full retirement" can be up to age sixty-seven. In order to enjoy one's retirement, you need to be in optimal health. Harold's stroke was a clear sign that health is to be coveted and attended to.

I did leave my career at KP "early" at age fifty-eight. Even though I left some money on the table, as they say, and we have to pay for health insurance until I reach sixty-five, it was simply time to go.

As my mom would say, "All money isn't good money." I enjoyed my thirty-three years with Kaiser; it was a wonderful company to work for, and I made lifelong relationships with both coworkers and patients, but the time was right to depart. You have to know when to say when!

Lesson #3: Find a fiduciary financial advisor and stick to the plan.

I mentioned this already but it bears repeating. I met with McIntosh Capital Management Company early in my career.

After doing the laborious homework, automatic monthly deposits into various accounts were set up. Automatic is the way to go so you don't really feel it, and it gets done without you having to do it yourself. And monthly, so you can see the money grow over time.

I didn't always like it because at times I felt I couldn't splurge, but I sure do appreciate it now being on the other side.

McIntosh Capital has crunched all the numbers and assures us that we will be comfortable until age one hundred, no matter what the stock market does.

Lesson #4: You don't need much. Live simply.

For our three-month journey, we lived out of two carry-on-sized suitcases apiece.

Instead of eating out all the time on the road, we would buy ready-to-eat things like salads and sandwiches from the grocery stores. Walmarts were everywhere and we got familiar with the layout of their stores.

Enjoying life isn't about accumulating stuff; it really is about relationships. It's about spending time with others. Stuff is replaceable, people are not.

We purged most of our belongings before the trip, keeping only our bedroom set, some dishes, two bookshelves, and clothing. What was left fit into a one-car garage space.

Lesson #5: Again, it's all about relation-ships.

We were on the road for eighty-one days! Of those, we spent only seven nights in hotels, a motel, and Airbnbs.

Mapping out the location of where our hosts lived helped to formulate our route. We have great friends and family who showered us with love and attention. They opened up their homes, took care of us, fed us, showed us around, and did not allow us to do much once in their homes.

To all of our hosts, we owe a deep, heartfelt thank you. This trip was not possible without your care and concern for us. We appreciate it all.

We cherish the memories, and we would love to re-pay the favor to you and anyone wanting to explore the world.

We drove over 8,000 miles in eighty-one days (from Harrison's birthday, also known as Valentine's Day, to Cinco de Mayo, now known as Amora's birthday, our newest niece) through eighteen states.

We only spent about $5,000 total in gas, food, lodging, and entertainment—everything.

Your thing doesn't have to be driving across the country or even traveling. But find what will bring you joy while you continue to thrive in your purpose. The end of one thing is the beginning of a new thing.

"For I know the plans I have for you, says the Lord. They are plans for good and not for evil, to give you a future and a hope."

Jeremiah 29:11 (TLB)

About the Author

Allyson Wynne Allen is freshly retired and an empty nester. After a fulfilling career as a pediatric physician assistant, she and her husband took the leap and sold everything to jump start their life after work. She plans on becoming a swim instructor, learning how to tap dance, and continuing to garden and volunteer.

Made in the USA
Columbia, SC
07 February 2025

52403163R00093